California *and* Back...

A Memoir by Martin Noble Hine

THIRD EDITION

Transcribed by George Noble Thompson
Edited by Adam Christopher Thompson
Book Layout & Design by Leslie Keats
Cover Design by Rafael Andreas

Opinions expressed in this book are solely those of the author
and do not represent the views of the publisher and editors.

californiaandbackbook@gmail.com

To my father, Blair Thompson

It is on his side of the family that I am related to Martin Noble Hine. I discovered these writings after I had a dream that I found an envelope full of papers in the old trunk at the foot of my bed. Upon waking up and searching through the trunk, I found these wonderful letters. I fondly recall stories my father told of his fascinating American family line, and only later in life have I come to appreciate such tales.

CONTENTS

PREFACE

In 1964, my grandfather George N. Thompson produced the first typescript of these original works by Martin N. Hine and submitted them to several magazines for publishing, to no avail. Unfortunately, I do not have the original handwritten documents, but am hopeful that this version will be another opportunity to tell Martin's story. Below is the cover letter my grandfather sent along with the work to the various publishers.

— Adam Thompson, San Francisco, California, October, 2019

"The following is a copy of an original hand-written letter presently in my possession. It is one of several accounts of the travel experiences of my great grandfather, who made the trip from Boston to California when 23 years of age.

Martin Noble Hine was born in Meredith, New York on November 15, 1829. He moved to Cannon, Michigan in November 1847 and went to California in 1852 and stayed through 1853, working as a carpenter and river boat trader in San Francisco and Sacramento. This stay in California is described in other letters, which have been preserved.

After returning by boat to the East, he met and married Lucy J. Tilton on October 21, 1855. She was born in Conway, Massachusetts on January 2, 1830. They had three children who were part of the seventh generation of "Hine" in America.

The earliest known Hine (or Hinde) was Thomas Hine, who came to this country as early as 1638 or 1639 from England. There appears no record of his age or birthplace, but he owned a house and lot in Milford, Connecticut on January 28, 1646, where he lived with his wife, Elizabeth, and their ten children.

However, our interest is in Martin Noble Hine, who many years later wrote of his life and wanderings."

George Noble Thompson
Marysville, California
February 13, 1964

Introduction

The story begins with handwritten letters owned by George Noble Thompson, great grandson of Martin Noble Hine. In 1852, Martin Noble Hine had traveled to California at the height of the gold rush to seek his fortune when he was 23. These three letters were the transcribed accounts of his adventure. Whether or not George Noble Thompson transcribed these accounts verbatim is unknown, as only the transcripts exist. The stories of this young man travelling to California in 1852, are exciting and compelling.

During those eighteen months, Martin witnessed several significant historical events: life aboard a ship that ran out of food, a stop at a port where he was marooned and introduced to the local culture, a stay in Sacramento where he survived cholera and typhoid fever and witnessed the 1852 fire and following flood.

On his return trip by way of Nicaragua, before the time of the Panama Canal, he and his fellow travelers had to cross the isthmus by mules in order to board a boat headed for New York. This trip was further complicated by a storm outside Norfolk forcing the crew to break up everything on board the ship to supply fuel to get them into port. Finally, Martin landed in New York, left the ship, boarded the New York Central Railroad and went home to live happily ever after.

1

Orange Groves, Mexico

The Orange Groves of Old San Blas
June 1852 – August 1852

Martin traveled from New York during the California Gold Rush. A great many ships making this run at the time were mail boats carrying mail, passengers, and goods from one coast to another. San Blas was a port in Mexico, along the route to San Francisco and the port at which many passengers changed ships. The barque "Emily" left Panama and put up at San Blas because of a shortage of supplies and food. The captain debarked and the passengers were left to their own resources. Although Martin makes light of the predicament, this journey becomes a personal memory of friendship and includes a dialogue that is found in the following chapters.

"Not yet astir? Why I believe you would sleep away a year's cruise if left to yourself!" says my joyful friend, Charles Foster, as he appears at my berth and rudely seizes me by the arm awakening me from a comfortable morning slumber. "This is our nation's anniversary," he continues, "and apostles though we are, some tribute is due to the memory of the deeds of our forefathers." "Yes indeed," I reply, "my dreams have already conveyed to me the scenes of those exploits, and but for your untimely interruption, I should probably have paid my tribute at the shrine of Liberty!"

California and Back...

"I am glad to find you thus early with your offerings," says he
smiling. "But dress yourself and meet me upon deck, where I will
propose to you a plan by which I mean to cheat at least one day
of its dullness! I am so weary of hearing the constant murmur
and of seeing faces portentous with self-inflicted sorrow that I
think a short absence would be a positive relief." Thus, saying, he
mounts the stairs and disappears upon deck where I join him. I,
too, have become so disgusted with the universal ennui that I am
glad to accept any proposal which will affect a change of scene.

About four weeks have passed since the "Emily," upon which
we are passengers bound for California, dropped anchor in the
harbor where we now lay, and the prospect of speedy departure
is daily becoming more doubtful. The few provisions purchased
upon our first arrival are nearly consumed and the Captain,
unable to procure more, has abandoned his ship, and taken a
temporary refuge in the interior. Such is our situation upon the
morning of July 4th, 1852, when we intrude ourselves upon the
notice of the reader, hoping that whoever may take the trouble to
follow us through this imperfect narrative, will pardon its errors
for the sake of the few "truths" it may contain!

It is the anniversary of our national independence, a day every
true American hails with joy! How many of my countrymen
would this day, gaze with pride upon the Stars and Stripes, the
emblem of a free and happy people. How many noble hearts
would break in emulation of the patriotism of their sires, are the

thoughts which occupy my mind. I mount the deck and run my eyes carelessly over the harbor where numerous vessels at anchor roll lazily over ceaseless swells and I see peeping from its forest of shrubbery, the rustic cottages which constitute a part of the little town of San Blas, Mexico.

Foster stands leaning against the mast with his eye fixed upon some distant object, apparently lost in thought, and does not notice my approach. He is one of those jovial merry heart fellows whose presence is a safeguard against melancholy, and whose sparkling witticisms and unheard-of philosophy is proverbial among his comrades of the vessel!

About twenty-two years of age, he has received all the benefits of a liberal education which adds to a mind naturally vigorous and retentive, raising him above the level of most persons of his age and circumstance. His light complexion and calm blue eyes always bear an expression of feminine softness, and no one is more conversant with him without discovering the fund of good humor which he always has in store. Our acquaintance has commenced upon the ship (where each finds himself destitute of acquaintance) and a friendship has sprung up between us, which at the time I speak, binds me to him as devoutly as a brother.

"Your thoughts must be of an interesting nature," say I, as I see a smile gather on his face. "Perhaps you are amused to find yourself practicing upon your own theory."

"You interrupted my reverie so untimely that I have entirely forgotten its purpose," says he, in answer to the first part of my query. "I confess it's easier to convince others of the utility of my philosophy than to practice it myself. However, I find but little difficulty in dispelling my drowsiness this morning."

"Doubtless, some tender recollection recalled by the return of another anniversary banished the drowsy god from your pillow!" I reply.

"The interest which I profess in the return of our nation's Independence Day is excuse sufficient to justify my departure from any usual custom," says he. "But come! Let me know your opinion of our proposed excursion."

"I will learn your plan before I approve," I reply.

"Truly, I had forgotten that you are ignorant of it!" says he, pointing to the old fort, which grey and somber stands in bold relief against the eastern sky. He continues, "For some time I have felt a great curiosity to see more of that old ruin than we have yet seen. There are many gloomy passages and dark halls there that I have never explored. Besides the old town is so quiet, that I have made up my mind to spend the day there. Will you bear me company?"

"Most certainly!" I reply. "But we must set out soon in order to avoid walking during the intolerable heat of midday."

In a short time, we are upon our way to the shore. Our vessel is anchored in the harbor about a mile from the landing. As the boat bears us over the intervening space, let me precede this by giving the reader an imperfect description of the scene through which he is requested to pass with us. Situated upon a low sandy point bordered upon the south by the sea and upon the west by the Grande River, is the little obscure town of San Blas. Its inhabitants are of the middle class of Mexicans, indolent and uneducated, subsisting almost entirely upon the spontaneous products of the soil.

Their dwellings are constructed of small poles, set in the ground and covered with a thatch roof of plantain leaves. Scattered through the town are majestic live oak trees, whose branches extend to an enormous length, affording a shelter to a large quantity of ground, so thick that the sun's rays never penetrate them. These trees are the only thing in or about the town which the stranger can find to admire. Beneath them, the natives sleep away the sultry hours of midday. In their shadows, the vendors of fruits dispose of their products. But San Blas, low as she now ranks in the world of enterprise, can boast of the wealth of her ancestors, of the nobility of their descent and of the faded beauty of their once loved home! That home is not the lowly hut where we now find them. Their ancestors are not the debased creatures which now represent them. Upon a rocky cliff about a mile down the coast from the place we have already described, stands the relics of the old town of San Blas! Leaving the shady grove and its indolent occupants, we pursue our way toward the scene of our day's excursion.

We cross a strip of desert land about half a mile in width, where nothing is visible save the savage-looking horseman, as he drives his ponderous spurs into the flanks of his jaded mule, and dashes at a gallop across the burning sand. We enter a little shady path which leads toward the ascent, reaching a point where the path winds along the side of the rugged acclivity separated from the broader one which continues along the base.

We seat ourselves upon a rock to rest a moment before attempting the ascent. Opposite to where we are seated, stands a monument of grey, free stones crowned with a huge cross. The half-consumed tapers stand around the statue and the rustic shelter which covers the whole, seems ready to fall from decayed pillars. The natives bow their heads as they pass this ancient structure, and consider it sacred, but from what cause I never was able to learn. Having sufficiently rested ourselves and seeing nothing to interest us where we are, we commence the ascent of the hill.

The narrow path cut in the rocks is steep and crooked and, in some places, almost inaccessible without the assistance of the thick growth of shrubbery which borders the path and shuts all other objects from view. We wind along the edge of precipices and look down upon the fields of broadleaved plantains that wave below, to see the few withered shrubs upon the plains which seem ready to ignite from the effects of the sun upon the burning sands.

The spire of the old cathedral is already visible above the impenetrable shrubbery, as soon we emerge upon the little plain which is the site of the old town and the scene of our present visit. Who has not at some moment of his headlong career passed in awe to gaze at some old uninhabited tenement, to roam through the silent halls once echoing the sounds of merriment and joy, and to breathe a sigh to the memory of those who passed their happy hours there? San Blas! Thou mournful relic of the past. Where now is the grandeur of those noble edifices, through which the mighty Aztec once proudly roamed? Where are the tablets engraved in memory of thy heroes? Who guards over thy deceased glories, or repels the invader from thy precincts? Who now wakes to the tones of thy bell in thy deserted cathedral, or offers a prayer within its portals? How changed! A few remnants of thy ancestry yet stalk about thy deserted streets like specters at midday, but the nobility of antiquity is not there.

Upon the extreme western part of the town stands all that remains of the ancient fort. The main building is encircled by an outer wall, high and thick (after the Spanish order) but is now broken in many places, and its top set with spikes and glass renders scaling it impossible. The gateway is open and unguarded and we pass through it and stand within the enclosure. The place is deserted! Not a human being save ourselves is visible.

Passing around the building, we come to its front where we can command the view of the sea. What a prospect. We stand upon a perpendicular rock and the waves of the sea break against its base hundreds of feet below. A feeling of dizziness creeps over me as I gaze down into the foaming waters and draw back in awe and admiration. The graveled walks are overgrown with weeds and the whitewashed walls are grey with the accumulated moss of years.

The harbor is before us, dotted with boats and the flags of the proudest nations of the globe float quietly over the scene. Among them I can discern the "Stars and Stripes," the emblem of my own loved country. And as I gaze upon the glorious banner, the semblance of which this day causes so many happy hearts to beat in unison. I feel proud of the title of American.

Charles stands with his arms folded across his breast, his fine countenance rendered doubly fascinating by the beauty of the scene which he beholds in the harbor. The decks of the American vessels are crowded with men, apparently in much agitation. And while we conjecture the cause of this commotion, the boom of the cannon breaks upon the stillness which is answered again and again until the whole lovely scene is enveloped in a wreath of smoke! One continuous shout is borne on the breeze of the morning echoes and re-echoes through the desolate halls and at last dies away in a faint murmur in the obscure chambers of the vanished proud race.

"Long may the Stars and Stripes wave over the land of the generous and brave!" bursts from the impassioned lips of Charles.

But the flush of enthusiasm which lights his face gives way to a sad expulsion as he thinks of his own situation and he adds musingly, "Happy, happy country and thrice happy people who can today gather round their own friends and bow before the altar of Liberty. But how is this?" he continues as he sees a shade of melancholy steal over my countenance. "Does the smell of Uncle Sam's powder act as an opiate upon you?"

"No, Charles, the sound of our country's cannon is not unwelcome to me. All my sympathies are enlisted with my countrymen, and tis the thought of my absence which makes me sad."

"We should not allow our thoughts to dwell too much upon home," says he, "while situated as we are here, or we should all become misanthropes."

"True, but everything which I see reminds me of home. Do not think me to be childish or homesick," say I, "but humor a caprice of which even you are not exempt. Give me excitement," I continue, "and I am of the indifferent, the most reckless. Give me danger and I can brave it without a murmur, but this insipid inactivity for months in such a place as this, is immeasurably tedious."

11

"Banish the sad impressions from your mind and let the future occupy your attention," says he, moving toward the old building.

"My memory is not of a nature to receive and discard impressions at my option," I reply, as I follow him.

We soon disappear in the interior of the crumbling ruins. For some time, we wander from room to room over the mass of rubbish, now stooping to crawl through doorways already half closed by the heaps of fallen mortar. Then, stopping to admire the monstrous columns which remain standing with nothing to support until we have made the circuit of the building. Occasionally a loosened stone from the arch falls with a hollow sound which echoes mournfully through the whole structure and startles the dank lizard in his retreat. And then all is again silent. Weary of witnessing the broken columns, the fallen arches and the crumbling ceilings, we enter a porch whose white-washed walls yet remain unbroken. There is carved the names of those who have previously visited the spot. We add ours to the number and hurry away glad to leave the foul atmosphere of the old ruins.

The cool breeze from the harbor travels invitingly among the groves of orange trees and the flowers from the neighboring thicket give forth a delicious odor while the silence which reigns throughout the deserted streets makes it a fit scene for meditation and repose and we throw ourselves upon the grass beneath the groves. I trace the course of the river by the reflected rays of the sun, as it winds through the mass of green shrubbery until it is hidden from view by the base of the distant mountain. I can see those gigantic forms whose tops are buried amid the floating clouds and trace its dark outline upon the aged vault until its misty shadow is lost in gloom.

Upon the plain, the herds are grazing on the short herbage and the town half buried amid its wealth of shade, seems as destitute of life as the ruins before us. Occupied with admiring a scene so beautiful and gathering the clusters of yellow bananas which hang temptingly over the wall of a neighboring grove, the hours speed rapidly by, and ere we are aware. The sun has passed this meridian and is fast descending the western sky. Surprised at the rapid flight of time we quit the grove and hasten to make the circuit of the town. Passing the prison-like walls of the old cathedral whose closed doors and somber aspect seem to deny admittance, we pass along paved streets teeming with rubbish. And through narrow alleys rendered nearly impassable by accumulated filth, we find ourselves in the eastern border of the town. Occasionally, we behold some aged native, like a specter of the past, peeping timidly forth from the tottering tenement, as if fearful that our footsteps will break the reigning silence or pollute a spot sacred to the fallen glories of the ages.

At a short distance to our right we discover a large stone edifice which is separate from any other building and seems to partake less of the dust of decay than any we have previously beheld.

Leisurely, we stroll along the half-overgrown path which winds among the trees approaching the edifice when our attention is arrested by strains of music issuing from the interior. We are about to retrace our steps lest our appearance might be considered an intrusion, when a man appears at the doorway and observing us, beckons us to follow him. He is of medium stature, apparently about sixty years of age. His long gray hair hangs sparsely over a brow wrinkled with the cares of many years and bears an aspect of much sorrow. Silently, we follow him through a long hall into a dark room in the eastern part of the building where he points to a rude bench and bids us, in Spanish, to seat ourselves.

Upon our first entrance, the room is so dark that I can scarce discern anything which it contains. But as my eyes gradually become accustomed to the darkness, as I look about me in mute surprise. Like all Mexican houses, the room is large, high, and the walls perfectly bare. Two narrow apertures serve for windows, that are nearly closed by the growth of shrubbery, admit all the light that enters the room. A few articles of old mahogany furniture are scattered about the room and in one corner, scarcely visible in the gloom, I discover a table upon which stands a box covered with black velvet. I have but little time to make observations upon the singularity of what I behold, for my attention is directed to the other occupants of the room. Besides ourselves and the old man who has led us hither, there are two other persons present. The one, a tall dark-complexioned man about 25 years old sits in one corner with a harp before him, the strings of which he occasionally touches mechanically, while his attention appears entirely engrossed in observing Charles and myself.

The other is a lady. She is seated near the table with her face concealed in her hands, apparently unconscious of our presence. She is dressed in a simple robe of white, which hangs loosely about the neck and half concealing the firmly molded shoulders and bosom over which the raven tresses hang in rich clusters. I cannot see her face, but her graceful form and the small delicate hand and rounded arm convinces me that she is a person of no ordinary beauty. While I meditate upon the probable cause of the sorrow which appears to infest the house (and which from my inability to speak Spanish, I am likely to remain ignorant of) the old man motions me to follow him and advances toward the table. Instinctively, I follow but as I approach the table the lady raises her head from her hands, and sees me, gives a slight start, then pushes back the disordered ringlets from her brow, and brushes away the tear which hangs upon her eyelids. She regards me with a look of mingled distrust and pleasure. Involuntarily, I stop and gaze upon the beautiful being before me. She is evidently about eighteen years of age, of a clear rich complexion and dark eyes which tell such volumes of sorrow that I feel all my sympathies enlisted in the beautiful girl.

She rises to her feet at my approach and I instinctively extend to her my hand which she unhesitatingly takes. During my strange introduction to the young lady, the old man removes the cloth from the box and I am horror struck as my eyes rest upon a corpse. It is the first intimation that I am in the chamber of death.

"Madre! Madre!" sobs the young lady as she presses her lips upon the inanimate brow of all that remains of her mother and then bursts into a fresh paroxysm of grief. The tears steal down the cheek of the old man, but he hastily brushes them away. Then as the music strikes up, he commences dancing around the body with demonstrations of joy. Horror struck at so unnatural a proceeding, I retreat to the opposite side of the room, and am about to leave the house when a motion from the young lady detains me. I have often heard of the ceremony among these people in preparing for the burial of their dead, but never before has the custom seemed to me so revolting. The old man continues to dance around the coffin, at times accompanied with a wild hollow laugh which echoes through the suite of rooms like a maniac's glee and then relaxes into sorrow as the melody changes from the animated to the plaintive. When the music ceases, he throws himself upon the coffin and gives vent to all the violence of his grief.

What Charles has been about all this time I know not, but turning toward him, I observe his eyes fixed upon the young lady with ill-concealed admiration. Unfortunately, neither of us understands sufficient Spanish to converse with them, and after remaining a few moments longer, we inform them by signs that we are about to leave them.

The old man extends his hand which I cordially press and with a bow to the young lady. And to my surprise, she rises and advances with us toward the door. Reaching the hall, she pauses and offers me her hand (which Charles says I carried to my lips) and in plain English repeats, "Goodbye." Toward Charles, she observes the same courtesy and disappears into the building.

Our eyes follow her retreating figure and a long-drawn sigh escapes the lips of Charles as we turn down the narrow path which leads to the entrance.

"What an angelic creature!" he exclaims when we are a short distance from the grove. "I can scarcely persuade myself that it is genuine flesh and blood which we have just beheld!"

"She is truly a beautiful being," I answer abstractedly, "possessing so much unaffected gracefulness and simplicity."

"Poor girl," he adds with a sigh. "Aye Charles, if eyes speak truth, the look of admiration which I detect in yours, tells a stranger tale." A slight blush is his only answer.

We join the boat crew and soon are upon our way to the ship. But each as we look back upon the old fort, upon whose top the last rays of the setting sun yet linger, are mentally resolved that this day's visit to the old ruins is not likely to be the last. Reaching the ship, I throw myself upon my berth and reflect upon the singular scene which I have witnessed and imagine I can hear the tones of the harp and see the grey locks of the old man as he danced around the coffin. I behold the sorrowful features of the lovely girl when first she raised her tearful eyes to mine and so gracefully offered me her hand at parting. Who is she, and how does she know the little English I have heard her use, are mysteries I am determined to solve, and I fall asleep.

Nearly two days have elapsed since our return from the old ruins, when this morning we find ourselves once more in that vicinity. The young lady is in the grove at the time of our approach and she welcomes us with a smile and motions us to a rustic seat under an orange tree where she soon joins us. Her countenance wears an expression of deep sorrow, yet a calmness supersedes the grief which she has experienced at the death of her mother.

Her name, she tells us, is Julie Moncalve, and that she has lived in that old town since she can remember, almost in obscurity, she says. A few years before when she was quite young, an English gentleman was a guest at her father's house for a short time and from him she learned all that she now knows of the language of our race.

Time has sped on and nearly every day finds Charles and me at the old town. None of our comrades have discovered the course of our frequent visits, and now we have taken up quarters ashore, and our absence has not been noticed. The time hangs heavily upon us amid the monotony of scenes in which we have so long mingled, that it is but natural for us to seek pastime in the inviting grove that surrounds the old cottage as we are charmed by the melodious voice of the dark-eyed señorita.

The half confidential, half timid air with which she always converses with us, renders her more interesting and her pure simplicity and ignorance of the world, makes her society always agreeable. Supplied with as proficient a teacher as my friend Charles, she acquires a sufficient knowledge of our language to converse with us quite freely. Yet there is just enough uncertainty with her, as to the appropriateness of the word she is about to make use of which renders her conversation amusing. Instead of feeling piqued at her mistakes, she joins us in the laugh they create, and again makes the attempt.

Toward me, she manifests a friendly reserve but toward Charles, I observe that her deportment is prompted by other feelings than mere friendship. With sorrow I perceive their growing intimacy as arm-in-arm I behold them strolling through the grove, her countenance beaming with pleasure as he details to her the stories of his native land, to which she listens with wonder and delight. As he presses his lips upon her radiant brow at parting, I tremble to think of the intensity of the passion which he is exciting in the bosom of that pure minded girl. Soon and hopelessly though, a golden dream of her life must be broken.

19

Charles sees the disappointment which he is preparing for her and pauses, but the silent look of reproach with which she meets him after an absence, and the pleasure he experiences in her society, overcomes his prudence, and again he becomes a daily visitor. I am his companion more from a sympathy for the fair Julie in the trial which I know is impending, than from any real pleasure I expect to realize from the visit.

The summons at last comes from the ship that we must be ready to embark upon the following morning. The announcement is hailed with joy by most of our comrades, who have become weary of our prolonged stay, but Foster's countenance wears an expression of sadness which I in vain try to dispel.

We set out for the old town when the news of our sudden departure reaches us. It is with sorrow that he reflects that this present is to be his last interview with the innocent Mexican girl. Too well aware of the nature of his thoughts to question him, we assume our journey in silence.

"So," says he musingly, "the dreaded time has come. Poor Julie, how lonely she will be when we are gone."

"Well may you say that," I reply. "Enshrouded as she is within the gloomy walls of that deserted town, who will pay homage to her virtues or mourn her death?"

"But, Charles," I continue, "have you no compunctions at leaving her now? You, who have thus ungenerously stolen all the affection of her confiding heart, you, whom she loves, with all the fervor which a heart that has never known love before is capable of loving. Forgive me," I add quickly, as I see a shade cross his brow. "Forgive my impetuosity, but I feel an interest in the fate of that young girl for which I cannot account. You have made a few days of your existence happy by your presence, at the expense of a lifetime of misery."

"It is rather for me to ask pardon," he says. "I have merited all your reproaches. Yet, believe me, I am not guilty of having wantonly trifled with her affection. I know the depth of her love. I know that for me she would sacrifice her life, her honor, and her eternal happiness and never have I been able to command my better nature enough to tell her that she must not love me. Oh, the restraint of a selfish world. I would prefer a life of obscurity cheered by the loving tenderness of this simple child of nature, above the cold formality of society decked with the gewgaws of fashion. But it must not be. The moment of separation has come."

"Have you never spoken to her of your departure?" say I, not a little touched by his sufferings.

"Never." he replies. "I never could think of paining her by an allusion to it, and of late my attention has been so much occu-

21

pied with my present happiness that I have had no thought of the future, until the message of today reminds me of it."

"Ahead," say I, "she is waiting for us," as I catch a glimpse of a white dress through the foliage. 'May Heaven protect her through her coming trial,' is my mental ejaculation. As with a countenance beaming with the freshness of morning, she hastens to meet us.

Extending to me her delicate hand, she smilingly bids me welcome and advances toward Charles, who stands regarding her with mingled feelings of love and pity. She clasps his hands within her own and gazes into his face with eyes that seem to read the sorrow of his heart. All the happy scenes which he has passed with her come in review before him, and the thought that he must leave her alone and unprotected is maddening, and he clasps her to his bosom and weeps.

Poor trusting Julie. She little dreamed of the bitter cup which was hers to drain. We are obliged to shorten our stay in order to make some preparation for the remainder of the voyage, and to avoid an interview which I have no inclination to witness. I retire to another part of the grove and amuse myself by taking a last look at what has become a familiar scene, a last look at a world of sorrow is embodied in these words. The weeping family, as they press the hand of the spirited man as he embarks on his return trip voyage, watches his figure to catch the last look, ere he is

23

borne from their view forever. The broken-hearted mother as the clods fall mockingly upon the coffin, bends forward to take a last look of all that is left of her darling child.

This is a place so lovely, so shrouded in quiet, it always awakes a sensation of pleasing melancholy whenever I chance to stray through its alleys unaccompanied. Now I am to leave it, the only spot that I am delighted to visit upon that western shore, the spot that relieves my hours from the contagion of sad reflections, the birthplace of that relic of Castilian nobility, the pure-minded Julie. And I will recall to memory the delicious coolness of that orange grove, the fragrance of the flowers fresh with the dew of morning, and the beauty and simplicity of its uneducated tenant, and involuntary sigh which memory awakens, escapes me.

The meridian sun reminds me that it is time for us to return, and I hasten to the spot where I left Charles and Julie. I find them seated side by side upon a rude bench and the agitated countenance and tearful eye informs me that she knows her fate.

"Oh Charles," she says, as she lays her hand upon his arm and looks into his face with an agony of despair. "Let me but hope that I will see you again, that you will someday return, though months or years hence and I will be happy."

"No, Julie, No. You must forget me. I cannot and will not deceive you. An agency over which I have no control urges me away. I have a destiny to fulfill which may separate us forever. But did you know the pain which this separation gives me, your generous heart would not accuse me."

"I do not, I do not accuse you, Charles," she says passionately. "It is only that I am to blame. How can I expect you to leave the home where you are so much loved, to leave your native country for an uneducated girl like me? Go Charles, go and be happy," she adds, turning away to conceal her emotion.

"Julie, Julie, you mistake me," he cries, clasping her hand. "Be my fate what it may, I will never cease to love you and when you look upon this (and he draws a ring from his finger and puts it upon hers) remember that the giver is faithful to his vow, though we never meet again." Plucking a rose, which she gives him, she replies with a sigh, "Unlike that fading token will be the love of Julie."

Unwilling to remain longer as a spectator of such a scene, I advance toward them. Julie blushes deeply and tries to conceal her confusion, but in vain. I take her hand and press it to my lips, but my heart is too full for utterance. She raises her tearful eyes to mine, and they bear the same expression of sorrow which I had seen in them when she sat by her mother's coffin. Without uttering a word, I press my lips upon her pale brow and hurry down the path. The tears stand in Foster's eyes as he approaches her. A moment she hesitates and then throws herself into his arms and

25

gives way to all the pent-up agonies of her heart. More I cannot witness; never after will I awaken the sadness of my friend by attending to the parting scene at old San Blas!

But a little more remains to be told. The vessel has been about three weeks at sea laboring against head winds, and the provisions are again getting scarce. Disease caused by a lengthy stay in a pestilent climate is daily thinning our number, and scarcely a day passes that does not add to the list of death. The sufferings are becoming insupportable. For some time, Charles has been unwell, but I apprehend no danger. I have been his constant attendant by night and day. Yet, I have never heard him allude to the place we have left, nor mention the name of Julie.

One afternoon I leave him with a friend for the purpose of taking a few moments' sleep, of which I stand in much need, expecting in a short time to see Charles recovered and about deck. I have not slept more than an hour, when I am awakened with the tidings that he is dying. Hastening to his side, I grasp his hand and call upon him to speak to me. He recognizes me and in a feeble voice pronounces my name and draws me closer to him as if he would speak with me.

"Julie," he says, gasping for breath. "Tell her..." and his voice dies away, his eyeballs roll in their sockets. A spasmodic quiver runs through his frame and he is dead. His destiny is fulfilled, the invisible agency has called his spirit from Earth.

Carefully preserved, I find a withered rose, which tells of his remembrance of the dark-eyed Julie. None save myself know of the tie that bound him to the orange groves of old San Blas.

Silently, I watch the preparations for his burial and as I gaze upon his corpse and review the scene through which we had passed since our acquaintance, I scarcely realize that the inanimate body before me is all that remains of the youthful and talented Charles Foster.

His body is carefully sewed in canvas and placed upon a plank on the deck. With bare heads, all gather around to pay the last tribute of respect to a loved comrade. The service is read, the plank raised, a splash follows and the blue waters bury him from our view forever. Among strangers he closes his brief career, where no mother smooths his dying pillow, or loved one weeps at his departure.

In about ten days the vessel anchors at San Francisco and the passengers disembark, and due to the constant bustle and excitement of California, the fate of their comrade is soon forgotten. Julie Moncalva, if she yet lives, is ignorant of the fate of Charles who for a short time converted the gloomy relics of old San Blas into a paradise.

The Levee and Steamers at Sacramento City
Lawrence & Houseworth, Publisher

A Short Residence in California
in the Early Days
September 1852 – October 1853

When Martin reached Sacramento, he probably fully intended to
complete his journey to the 'Gold Rush' region. But natural disas-
ters of floods and fires and health epidemics of smallpox, cholera,
and typhoid fever robbed him and many of his fellow travelers of
reaching their desired destinations. Life was tough, but Martin survived through his building talents and his ability to connect with
people who needed a young, energetic, resourceful and personable
helpmate. Back in San Francisco, his port of entry, he reaches his
limit and heads for home.

September 12th, 1852, I have arrived at Sacramento, California,
where I am so fortunate as to find here the family of S.M. Harrison of Grand Rapids, Michigan. They had crossed the Plains,
starting three months later than I and have been in Sacramento
keeping a boarding house two months before my arrival. I stop at
their boarding house, working for my board until I become able
to do something else.

My ordinary weight is 160 pounds, but when I landed in
California, I weigh less than ninety pounds, my clothes are all
worn out or quite ragged and I have only a $2.50 gold piece in my
pocket. The boarding house is on the second story over a store on
J Street and the sleeping room is fit up with berths, ship fashion,
and about twenty boarders are lodged in that one room.

29

One night, one of the lodgers is sick and a physician is called in the early morning who pronounces it a case of smallpox. We are all vaccinated and quarantined in the room with the smallpox patient for two weeks, but not one of the other lodgers gets the disease, although the patient comes out badly pitted.

Sacramento is built upon low, level ground at the confluence of the Sacramento and American Rivers, the banks of which are diked with a levee six or eight feet above the bank and twenty or more feet wide, to protect the city from the annual floods of the river. The climate is delightful in the summer season, when for months not a cloud obscures the sun, and the snow-clad Sierra Nevadas glisten in the sunlight on the faraway horizon. About the streets, the people clad in linens, where they pursue their accustomed avocations, or promenade for pleasure. The days are sometimes a little too warm, but the nights are always cool and pleasant.

There is no railroad to Sacramento and all communication with the outside world is by the river. As Sacramento is the main distributing point to the mining regions, an immense amount of freight is daily brought in by the San Francisco boats, there being two opposition boats each way every day, besides a line of regular freight boats. Nothing in the provision or merchandise line is produced in the country so the entire supply is brought from the Atlantic States, South American or Mexican coast.

From Sacramento, the supplies for the mining regions are loaded into huge wagons drawn by six large sleek looking mules with plaited harnesses, guided by one line in the hands of a rider on the back of the off-wheel mule. Sacramento is a busy town. Caravans of merchandise are hourly leaving for the mines. People are coming in crowds, and reports of new discoveries of gold are every day heralded about.

The gambling houses are the most conspicuous and the best frequented places in the town. Many a poor miner with the accumulation of two hard years of labor in the mines is enticed by the music from the gambling halls where he drops his sack of gold dust and returns penniless to the mines again. Many of these are on their way home to the states with means enough to make their families comfortable and all of it is swallowed up in a single night.

The town is well laid out with broad streets, named alphabetically one way, and numerically the other, but most of the buildings are two-story wood structures unflustered, but lined upon the inside with sheeting and papered over that. It is a model of hastily constructed towns that have sprung up since the gold discoveries of California.

After a time, I am able to work and secure a job at my trade and work about three weeks at $7.00 per day. I buy a chest of tools and some decent clothes and begin to feel very well contented with my surroundings, when I am taken down with the cholera. For two weeks confined to my bed. There is no fun in having the cholera, I am quite certain. After getting past the danger line, I can only go bent, nearly doubled over, and am in that condition when the big fire breaks out that destroys nearly all of the city.

The fire starts just opposite my lodgings and fans the heavy wind that leaps across the street in a moment and goes sweeping on like a whirlwind. I barely have time to get on my pants and boots and seize a blanket and get out when the fire sweeps all through the building. All my bedding, clothes and tools go up in smoke. In my condition, I can just manage to keep out of the way of the billows of flame and frequently find my retreat cut off by flying cinders lighting fires ahead of me.

In less than three hours' time, the whole city is laid in ashes, except for a few scatterings housed on the extreme outskirts. So rapid is the work of destruction that nothing is saved. The city fire engines are abandoned and burned in the streets. Piles of merchandise and household goods are taken from the buildings only to be licked up by the devouring flames outside.

Over 600 buildings and over $5,000,00 worth of property is burned. The morning after the fire, 10,000 homeless people without food are wandering where the streets have been, and more are searching among the drifting ashes for treasures lost in what had been their homes. Everyone is blackened by the smoke and ashes, and one hardly recognizes a familiar acquaintance.

Many of the people take boats to other towns or strike out to the mining regions. Provisions soon come flowing in. Tents are hastily erected, and the work of rebuilding soon begins. As soon as lumber can be brought in, wooden structures begin to go up all over the burned district. From among my burned tools, I find a square, saw and hammer and with these, I help put up the first building. None of the other workmen having any tools except those picked up among the ashes.

It is getting near the time of year for the commencement of the rainy season and everyone is in a hurry to get housed before it commences. Wages go up to $10 per day and every carpenter in town is in good demand.

Mr. Harrison has early gotten up a tent and all his old boarders have come back. Through the center of the tent, we arrange a table upon stakes driven in the ground and berths along the sides covered with canvas.

About the middle of December, the rain began to come down in torrents. I've never before seen such a rainfall. For over ten days there is no let-up and the whole country is deluged. The water in the rivers raises rapidly and stands several feet above the streets of the city, shut out by the levees.

On December 31st, the levee gives way two miles below the city, and the water rushing through the break flows back into the city, until there is not a foot of land in the whole town that is not two to twelve feet under water.

Such a New Year's I've never seen before and hope never to see again. People are wading about the principal streets up to their armpits in water. Everything that could float is brought out.

Wagon boxes are caulked, hogsheads are sawed in two and the streets present a carnival of floating craft. Every few moments someone's craft comes to grief and the occupants go floundering in the water. Everyone who has a second story flees to it and those occupying tents pull them down and strike for higher land. Business of all kinds come to a dead standstill.

Up to this time, I have been staying at Harrison's tent, but after the rainy season sets in, we have anything but an agreeable time. The soft mud beneath the tent is fully six inches deep and the water leaks through the canvas into our berths until all our blankets are saturated. Half a pailful of water frequently settles in the canvas bottom of our berths. If we take off our boots and stand them by the side of our berths, someone is sure to knock them over and in the morning, we find them filled with mud and water.

With three other young fellows, I find a chamber room in the outskirts of town that the fire has not reached and we rent it, move in, and keep bachelors' hall during the balance of the winter. The water stands within a foot of the chamber floor and we have to clamber in and out through the window, but we are more comfortably housed than most of the people. One of my mates and I get bench room upon one of the old hulks laying at the Sacramento levee.

We open up a shop where we do quite a thriving business building small boats, fish boats and repairing damaged steamers. Neither of us are practical ship carpenters but we manage to turn out some first-class boats and do the repairing on the steamers to the satisfaction of the parties concerned.

The water gradually recedes. But it is a month before the most elevated streets are bare and then so soaked and muddy, that a team will almost sink out of sight if it attempts to go over one of them.

Six months from the time of the inundation, the water has not receded from the lowest parts of the city and small boats from below are within two blocks of the main street of the city. For forty miles below Sacramento, on the south side of the river, there is a low swale several feet below the banks of the river and each year this swale grows an immense crop of tules (an overgrown bull rush) which shoots up twelve to fifteen feet high and so dense that it is difficult to force a passage through them. The backward flow of water gathers these dead tules and floats them back to Sacramento where they cover the ground eight to ten feet deep.

The sidewalks have all been burned by the fire and there is no way to get about town after the water recedes but to wade through mud. Some enterprising genius has attached a small mule to a flat-bottomed boat which slides along nicely in the soft mud and he does quite a freighting business. I have seen finely dressed ladies seated in this boat riding through the mud on their way to or from the steamers.

While engaged in boat building, I make the acquaintance of Dr. H.B. Rice, a former resident of Arkansas. He is building a scow covered boat for the purpose of trading with the people living along or near the river. I help him to build the boat, which is forty feet long and twelve feet wide, all covered except a platform at the bow where row locks are affixed, and a capstan attached.

The front end of the boat is arranged with counter and shelving open on one side and about twelve feet of the stern is occupied by his family consisting of a wife and little boy. The boat is built after the plan of the trading boats so common on the Arkansas River. I become quite interested in the enterprise and finally persuaded to take an interest with him and help stock and manage the boat

On April 12, we have the boat ready and stocked up when the family comes on board and we cast off the lines and float with the current down the turbid Sacramento. Upon the upper deck we have a mast that can be raised or lowered and a square sail to help us make the ascent of the river, the current of which is strong and the stream in many places very crooked.

36

Sometimes, we sail along quite nicely but then we strike a stretch of water where the wind will not blow, or blows from the wrong direction. This is when we have to run out a long line ahead and wash the boat up by means of the capstan. Going downstream is easy enough, for we float with the current and steer the craft with a long oar at the stern of the upper deck.

We have a long bugle-like horn which we use to blow, and which can be heard from two or three miles. The people along the river soon get to know it and come flocking into our landings. Forty miles below Sacramento, the river divides to form two channels, the old river makes quite an oxbow circuit, but the new channel (or slough as it is called) cuts across the peninsula. This is a deep narrow cut about six miles long through which the main part of the river rushes with a strong current. Through this slough all the steamers pass, but we go down the old channel and come back through the slough.

There are two rival lines of steamers that are always racing. I have seen them come down the river at full speed and turn into the slough side by side under a full head of steam. Here the two boats completely fill the channel, the waves wash over the river-banks six to eight feet high. It is no common thing to see one of the boats come out of the slough minus a wheelhouse.

We always have to watch the coming of the steamers and get where we can swing the stern of our boat into the stream and hold it off the shore. If we get caught broadside to the banks, the waves throw down everything in our storeroom.

We keep a stock of dry groceries, notions, a few dry goods, boots and shoes and frequently take orders for articles that we do not carry. It takes us about two weeks to make the trip and after the first two trips, our trade has so increased that I have to go to San Francisco each trip to stock up. I catch a steamer at Twin Islands (the lower end of our route) and I am in San Francisco in the morning where I make my purchases and take them back with me on the steamer in the evening, losing only one day's time.

Life upon our boat is not without its amusing and exciting features and we form many pleasant acquaintances with the people along the river. The head of the slough is one of our landing places and we frequently remain there two days. Upon one side of the river is Runyon's Ranch and upon the other is Robbs' Ranch. Mrs. Robb came to California as a member of the famous Alleghanians and married after arriving there. She has her piano and is a fine singer and we spend many evenings in her pleasant parlor.

The storeroom is my dressing and sleeping room where I have a mattress that I put upon the counter nights, and let down a curtain of mosquito netting which I carefully tuck in all around me. I have seen mosquitos in some of the most famous mosquito countries, but for size, quantity or persistency, I think Sacramento Valley after a flood would take the premium on able bodied mosquitos.

One day we leave our landing at Robbs' Ranch and attempt to sail up the river, but the wind is in the wrong quarter and drifts us into the overhanging trees. After making a half mile or more, we conclude to drop back to our anchorage, but the wind blows so strong that it drives our boat upon the shore. I jump ashore and with a long tule pole hold the boat off and let it drop down the stream. The water is muddy and, in some places, comes over the bank so that I have to wade and in one of these I go into a deep hole and get thoroughly soaked.

When we reach the landing, I get behind the counter to put on some dry clothing. I have just got fully stripped when Mrs. Robb and two or three other ladies appear on the platform. I dodge under the counter and the doctor [Dr. Robb] waits on the customers. He manages to entertain the ladies so well that he keeps me cramped beneath the counter naked for an hour or more.

It is fun for the doctor, but no fun for me as I expect any moment that he by some pretext will get some of the ladies behind the counter. I watch for a chance to pay the doctor off for that trick, and it soon comes.

We are tied up for the night at a landing a few miles up the river and he goes ashore to gather wood. A dry limb on a sycamore hangs over a deep slough and in attempting to get it, he loses his balance and plunges headlong into the slough. He cannot swim a stroke, but I manage to fish him out. He always has a huge cud of tobacco in his mouth and in making the plunge he has swallowed the cud.

A sicker man I never saw. While he tries to get on some dry clothing in his family room, some ladies call, and I send them right into the room. The doctor just has time to hide behind the bed where he has to remain until the ladies take their departure. He is sick as a dog, but not daring to make a sign to reveal his hiding place.

We have no water to use but what we get from the river is so muddy that in every tumbler full, there is a quarter inch of mud settled at the bottom. I remain upon the river about three months, when I have an attack of typhoid fever which lays me up, and the doctor gets a man in my place to help run the boat.

One day they are sailing up the river, the doctor steering and managing the sail, and the new man standing on deck with a long tule pole to shove the boat from the overhanging branches, when he makes a false movement and goes overboard. I am lying upon my couch below with a burning fever upon me, but I hear the splash and have sense enough left to now realize the situation, and I spring to the platform, plunge into the river and carry the fellow ashore.

He cannot swim a stroke and the doctor cannot leave the helm to assist him. By the time we reach the shore, the boat is twenty rods away and if I had not gone to his assistance, the fellow would doubtless drown. Instead of doing me any damage, I think the bath is a decided benefit to me as my fever abates from that time.

My attack leaves me feeble and subject to frequent attacks of chills and fever, so I conclude to leave the river and go to San Francisco, still retaining my interest in the boat. The doctor will send orders to me and I will ship him the goods and I have some tools and can work at my trade when I am able to do so.

My old boat building partner, D.R. Evans, has come to San Francisco and I first get a job on the [U. S.] Marine hospital, then building on Rincon Point, but afterwards go in with a contractor and help to build several dwelling houses. The chills and fever still hang about me and every week or two I have to lay by with it. I'm having one of these attacks when one day I go down to the wharf to see the New York steamers off. There is a big crowd of people about and excitement is running high. The opposition lines have got to cutting rates and the agents are upon the wharf selling tickets to New York for $10 each.

A "home fever" gets hold of me in a moment, and I hunt up my employer and tell him that I am going home and want my pay. He tells me that he cannot get the money for me for about two weeks and that I need have no fear of rates advancing before the leaving of the next steamer. He offers to pay the difference in rates if there should be an advance. I have previously sold my interest in

41

the trading boat to the doctor which I had deposit in the bank of Wells Fargo & Co. and my employer is owing me over $200.

The steamers from New York to San Francisco arrive and depart every two weeks, and I go to work again to wait for the next steamer. In the meantime, I dispose of my tools and make all preparations for leaving. The papers are filled with notices and every conspicuous place is covered by posters announcing the low rates of fare, and people from all over the state are coming in crowds to get the benefit of the cut rates, but none of the offices are open for the sale of tickets.

For two or three days, I make life a burden to my employer but only get promises that I should have my pay before sailing day. But the day of sailing, he cannot be found, and I've lost my wages.

The day before one of the steamers leaves, the ticket offices open and the lowest fare to New York is $250. I have sacrificed in the sale of my tools, done ten days extra labor, lost $270. that my employer owes me and pay $240. more for my ticket than it would have cost two weeks before. The increase of rates shuts out many, who return angry and disappointed to the mining regions again. I leave my claim with my friend Evans for collection, but he is never able to get any of it. He can't even collect the pay for his own labor and loses more than I.

Thus ended my experience of thirteen months in California. I never visited the mining regions, never saw the big trees of the Yosemite Valley, had never been in the fertile valley of the San Jose, or seen the rich fruit lands of the Los Angeles or San Bernardino County. But what I do know of California would fill a good size volume.

US Mail Steamship "Pacific"
from an original lithograph by Day & Son

Returning from California
October – November 1853

Martin's trip back home was no easier than the one to California.
His descriptions of his return journey are historically enlightening
as he tells of this time before the Panama Canal was built and Nicaragua was the primary port for travel between the eastern and western United States. This was also an extraordinary time in American history as California had just achieved statehood. Many events
happened almost simultaneously with the discovery of gold, leading
some to wealth and others to despair. Martin's recollections capture
the essence of this most challenging time.

At 4 o'clock Saturday Oct. 1, 1853, the steamer "Pacific" casts off
the lines from its San Francisco wharf, the wheels begin to move,
and the boat swings into the bay, turning the point of Telegraph
Hill, and moving down the harbor toward the ocean. From the
dock as the steamer swings away, comes the cheers of the multi-
tude there assembled to see us off and bid us farewell and God-
speed before our journey. Among them I can see many familiar
faces (of friends, perhaps of short acquaintance, but nonetheless
genuine) who have come to give me a parting salutation.

How different the appearances and expressions of the passengers from those who I had seen embark from New York less than
two years before. That crew was largely made up of soft-handed,

standing collar, plug-hat men who have left home and friends, on an uncertain mission, full of hardships and dangers, in a far distant country, perhaps to meet the loved ones no more on earth. These are men of the same class, perhaps some of the same who had taken a hard lesson in the world's school, who with pants tucked into high boots, in red or blue flannel shirts and slouched hats with horny hands, long hair and full beard and revolver and bowie knife strapped around them, are starting with joyful anticipations upon their homeward journey to meet their loved ones once more.

While life in California has changed the external appearance of these men, has made them look rougher and courser, it has also made them more charitable and more generous by bringing them into contact with a new class of people. It has often been said that an old Californian would divide his last crust with an unfortunate stranger. My experience among these people confirms the encomium, for I have never known a more generous hospitable people. Money comes easy and goes freely.

Our steamer is commanded by Capt. Blethen [Blethan] of the ill-fated "North America" [wrecked en route from San Juan del Sur, Nicaragua to San Francisco; with all 995 passengers saved] and is leaving the coast with the greatest number of passengers ever carried eastward from San Francisco. With a smooth sea, we pass down the harbor, leave the Golden Gate behind us, and before the shades of night close down, are well out to sea, but not out of sight of land. During the next three days, the wind is fresh, but the sea is not rough, and we get fairly settled down to the routine of life on shipboard. Novel reading, card playing, and sleeping are the principal occupations, while some lounge aimlessly about the boat and yet others make themselves troublesome and obnoxious by too liberal a patronage of the saloon. We are out of sight of land and the weather has become perceptibly warmer and shirt sleeves or linens have taken the place of heavy woolens.

The fourth day out we pass the Island of Guadeloupe and the sixth day, the high bluffs of Capo St. Lucos [Cabo san Lucas] which are shrouded in clouds but both at too great a distance for us to discern anything on shore. It seems as if all the drunken rowdies of California have got on this boat and it being so crowded, they cannot find a place to sleep. They spend the nights in drinking and making such a noise that no one else can get any sleep. The first night out one of them falls overboard and is lost, and the sixth night another shares the same fate. No one seems to know who they were, and their fate will always remain a mystery to friends awaiting their return.

We are nearly opposite San Blas, and as memory recalls, the agony of suspense that I experienced in this antiquated Mexican town, and the sufferings and dangers encountered upon these death-laden waves, I cannot but wonder that I am still among the living.

47

California and Back...

The air is oppressively hot and not a breath of wind stirs the glassy surface of the water. Involuntarily, I am watching the horizon for some sail craft laden with starving people whose vessel is rolling lazily upon this calm sea and the burning sun pouring its heated rays upon their death-laden vessel. On board the steamer we are all driven below or beneath the awnings during the day, but as the sun sinks into its watery bed, the air cools suddenly and the crowd is again astir and active.

We are nine days from San Francisco and are weaving down the coast with the rocky cliffs and lofty mountains in full view. These mountains are very beautiful ones. From the water's edge they rise like heaped-up broken columns, while back higher and still higher rises the craggy tops until their summits are lost in the lowering clouds.

The rocky bluff, the dark ravines, the cactus burdened vale alternate with the view. The rays of the setting sun cover the mountain side with a golden halo while a huge rainbow hangs like an arch above.

The poet tells us "There is beauty in stories," but that depends much upon the conditions in which we see them. Today these mountains are a beautiful picture as I sit upon the deck and watch the gorgeous panorama, but I remember when once a shipload of starving men approached this shore and finding here nothing to satisfy cravings of hunger and thirst, turned despairingly away without one thought of the sublimity of the picture. The picture then was just as beautiful as now, but we are in no condition to appreciate it. If the mountains had been solid gold and their peaks studded with diamonds, they would have been valueless to us as they furnished no relief to our necessities.

After six hours waiting for daylight outside the harbor of Acapulco, we enter at 7 A.M. and drop anchor about a half mile from the shore. The mail steamer "Panama" upward bound arrives two hours later. I had anticipated a run about the town and am much disappointed that owing to the prevalence of yellow fever in the place, none of us are allowed to go on shore. All our observations, therefore, must be made from the deck of the steamer.

Acapulco is one of the old Mexican towns with a population of about 4,000 and during the Spanish dominion in Mexico was the focus of the trade from China and the East Indies. Now it has since relapsed into conservative insignificance and is only a coaling station for the Pacific steamers. The opening of other ports now accessible to the interior and the railroads connects it with the States, and has diverted the trade and left the once-flourishing town in obscurity. Notwithstanding, it furnishes one of the best harbors on the Pacific coast.

From where the steamer is anchored, the outlet is entirely shut out from our view, and the harbor resembles a circular lake something like a mile in diameter entirely enclosed by green covered hills and forming a scenery quite beautiful and romantic. The town has but little to boast of in architectural pretensions, being built (like rural Mexican towns) without regard to order. Buildings seem to have been erected where the builder could find the best locations at all sorts of angles and no thought had been made of such unnecessary things as streets. Most of the buildings are low and built of stone covered with tile, but the outskirts I observe many of the cane huts so common in the country.

Two cathedrals (one of them in ruins) are conspicuous and the old cracked bell continually ringing is discordant enough to ruin the nervous system of a mule. If I were obliged to live within the sound of that bell, I should most devoutly pray that the good saints would take it into their holy keeping and remove the clapper.

There is a good deal of taste displayed in the cultivation of shade trees, and from the steamer's deck, I observe among them the palm, cocoa, orange, lemon and many other varieties that I am not familiar with. A fort surrounded by a nice grass plot stands upon a point defending the entrance to the harbor, but it shows no marks of warfare, save one hole opened by the only shot fired at it during the war. As a defense to the city, it is of doubtful utility.

A few weeks before our visit an earthquake had tumbled into ruins some of the most substantial buildings and fearful of a recurrence, many of the people are living in tents outside of the city.

50

Two or three of full-grown steers are taken on board our steamer and the process of loading is a cruel one. They are forced into the water to swim out to the steamer alongside boats where a pulley is attached to a yardarm and a rope attaches to their horns and they are drawn up a distance of twenty feet or more to the upper deck. They kick, bellow and pound air, but are safely landed upon the deck, apparently no worse for their neck stretching. I expected that their necks would be surely broken.

The water where we are anchored is fifty feet deep or more and so clear, we can easily see the pebbles at the bottom. A score or more of native boys from eight to twelve years old are constantly swimming about the steamer and we throw a nickel or dime into the water to see the little rats dive for it. As soon as the piece strikes the surface, the whole squad bends over and goes down like bullets, but they never fail at getting it, although many times they follow it to the bottom. The little fellows seem just as much at home in the water as on the land and they keep their places in the water as easily as if they are amphibious animals.

The "Panama" replenishes its stock of coal and is due to leave at 4 o'clock, but we spend the whole day while the vessel loads and it is not until 8 o'clock PM, when the anchor is raised and we steam out of the harbor. For three days following, there is a succession of fair winds and squalls with nothing occurring outside the ordinary routine of life on shipboard to interest us except the seasickness of many of the passengers.

51

At noon on the 14th day we land at San Juan del Sur and are
glad to place our feet on land once more. There is nothing that resembles a harbor and the steamer drops anchor a half mile from
the shore. We take small boats for the shore but most of them
run aground ten rods or more from the landings and we wade
the balance of the distance or get upon the back of some swarthy
native. I have seen too many fellows get a ducking while embark-
ing at Panama to relish that sort of a conveyance, so I gather up
my traps, climb over the sides of the boat and wade ashore only
half soaked while those that take the ride are generally fully im-
mersed.

What there is of San Juan has grown up since the opening of
the Nicaragua route to California. Consequently, the buildings are
newer and of a better quality than those of rural towns upon the
coast, but the place has no importance except as a landing place
for California passengers from whom the residents derive their
entire support. It happens at times that the Pacific steamers are
delayed and passengers from the states are detained here several
days, in which case the residents of the town reap a rich harvest.

The principal business of the people is furnishing transportation to the passengers to and from Pinda City (or Virgin Bay) for
which we all hold a ticket from the steamship company. Consequently, there is no chance for bartering or extortions. Upon
reaching the shore, we find hundreds of horses and mules ready
saddled from which we are to make selections.

They are a sorry looking lot, poor as snakes, hipped, spavined, sore backed, blind and invariably vicious, and whichever one a fellow selects, he is sure to wish before he reaches his journey's end that he had selected any other one. They are all professionals in the tricks of their business. One might as well shut his eyes and grasp the first bridle that is thrust into his hand as to attempt to choose from among them. To hear the owners extol the virtues of their animals, one would suppose them all as docile as sheep.

We take our baggage with us on the backs of the animals or hire a mule for its transportation and when mounting we are a motley-looking crowd. There are quite a number of women in the crowd who have to side straddle the same as the men. Every one of them is loaded down with baggage, and when satchels and parcels and board boxes and all other varieties of traps and calamities are strapped on, and the women encases herself among them, the animal is completely out of sight except its ears and a few inches of its legs. I do not wonder at the discouraged looks of the animals when they see that caravan of goods and livestock being strapped upon him. Happy at such a time is he who is flying light.

Some of the mules balk at the outset and neither coaxing nor pounding has the least effect upon them. Others start off at a rattling pace and the riders guy and laugh at their unfortunate neighbors upon the balky ones, but the beasts only wait their time and within the first two miles many are found stalled at the roadside, their mules laying down and trying to roll themselves out of their promiscuous loading.

53

One elderly lady weighing at least 200 pounds is passed about three miles out, and she is as complete a picture of despair as I ever behold. She is standing by the roadside and her little mule has lain down and is rolling upon the contents of the luggage upon the offside. Some men stop and assist her to get the mule upon his feet and her upon his back, when he immediately lays down upon the near side, dumping the old lady into the chaparrals and smashing all the baggage upon that side. If the old lady was a member in good standing of any orthodox church, it is well for her that her pastor was not one of our party, or she might have to account for the use of some words not defined in the church decalogue.

Notwithstanding the many annoyances, I never see a more jolly lot and never have more fun than during that ride from San Juan del Sur to Virgin Bay.

I am fortunate in my selection of a mule, not because I am posted in mule-ology, for I had never been on a mule's back before in my life. But I think the animal feels grateful to me for the small amount of baggage I burden him with for he never balks once during the trip. The only mulish trick that he serves me is by bolting out of the path under a thorn tree and scraping me off over the crupper. I catch at the limbs to save myself but instantaneously my hands are covered with an insect that seems to be a cross between an ant and a wasp. While they look like ants, the bite feels like the sting of a wasp. I presume I am the first real live Yankee that they have ever had a bite of, and they all sample me. For the next 24 hours my hands are swollen like a puff ball.

The path for most of the distance seems through a dense forest and I can see scores of monkeys swinging from limb to limb in the trees over my head, chattering in their monkey dialect and hear the half articulate voices of the parrots from the thickets and the song birds flitting from tree to tree.

The bushes bordering our path are laden with flowers and the forest is vocal with song. There is no reason why a good carriage road should not be built here as there are no topographical difficulties in the way. Such a road would cost no more than one for the same distance anywhere in Michigan.

A carriage road however might cost more for the country is doubtless like Mexico where the duty upon a carriage is sometimes as much as its original cost. In passing beyond the boundaries of Mexico into those of Nicaragua, we have not yet reached a country where the people have more political freedom or are granted more religious indulgences. They are equally ignorant, and priest ridden.

My mule brings me to Virgin Bay about five o'clock in time to secure good accommodations, but others of the party come straggling in during most parts of the night. Some of them may not have got over at all, for I do not remember seeing the fat old lady after leaving her at the roadside.

Virgin Bay (or Pinda City) is located upon the northwest shore of Lake Nicaragua and is one of the finest locations for a town that I have seen. The shore of the lake is high and the ground in the rear rises to the height of 100 feet in half a mile, offering a fine view of the lake, but the buildings are stuck in haphazardly like an Indian camping ground. One never knows which is the front and which the rear end of a building.

The people are civil and quite intelligent. Some of the senoritas are almost beautiful enough to steal the hearts of the young Americans and they act as if they would as soon do it as not. I could conceive of a life more unbearable than to settle right down here and enjoy a perpetual *dolce far niente*.

Lake Nicaragua is 110 miles long and 46 feet broad in its widest part and has an elevation of 120 feet above the waters of the Pacific. Mount Amatepe (an extinct volcano) rises from the lake about ten miles distant from the town but does not look to be more than two miles distant. Looking at it from Virgin Bay it appears like an artificial cone extending high heavenward.

The mountain is really in two distinct parts, both extinct volcanoes and nearly twenty miles long, but from our point of view we can only see one end of it. I see a thunder shower pass over it and from the shore I can see the top of the mountain glistening in the sunlight, while its base is obscured by heavily laden rain clouds.

Three small steamers are in waiting, and at 2 P.M. we embark, then arrive some time in the night at San Carlos, a fort at the head of the San Juan River and remain until daylight. The general impression among the passengers is that we are waiting for His August Majesty, the mosquito king, to finish his nap, and get a pass down the river through his dominions. Later observations convince me that our wait is for daylight to make the passage down the river which is so rapid that it could scarcely be navigated in daylight with safety.

The delay is not without its compensations for in the early morning we see the military display of the king's troops. There are about 100 of them in line upon the shore, a bare-footed dirty ragged looking lot of rascals armed with muskets that are dangerous only to those at the butt of them. I want to see some of our boys fire a revolver into the air just to see the rascals run. Upon the dock of our boat are the packages of gold dust shipped from San Francisco to New York, guarded by ten of these barefooted soldiers. One determined man could have cleaned out the whole posse of them.

About twenty miles from the head of the river, we come to the head of the rapids where we change boats, getting upon one that is so crowded that we hardly have standing room and in this, we go shooting down the foaming rapids for the next ten miles, dodging half submerged rocks and driving through channels that seem too narrow for the boat's passage. Those Nicaraguans are

57

good at steering a boat if they are good for nothing else, for they take us through without an accident and we reached Castillo at 12 P.M. and change boats again.

How these boats can ever make the passage of those rapids is more that I can conceive. It will come down fast enough and easy enough if properly guided but to get up through that whirlpool, where the water seems to be running at least 10 miles per hour, must require a good deal of steam power.

At Castillo we stop for dinner and the table looks really tempting, but every dish is seasoned with garlic or some other unpalatable stuff, that satisfies my appetite regardless.

Below Castillo, the river is very crooked and bordered by a thick growth of shrubbery and drooping trees. Over our heads, birds with rainbow plumage fly back and forth across the river, and in the heated air the perfume from the millions of flowers along the banks is fairly sickening. In turning one of the short curves, we encounter an upward bound steamer and the boats come together broadsides with a crash. Both are stern wheelers with guards about three feet wide on either side, even with the lower deck.

Our boat being the heaviest loaded, the guard of the other slides over that of ours and makes a scattering among the passengers standing upon the guard. One sick man lies upon his blanket upon our guard and is caught and instantly killed. I save my legs

58

by crawling through a cabin window and feel very thankful that the window happens to be there and open.

We arrive at Greytown (San Juan del Norte) in the evening and immediately go on board the "Northern Light" without making any explorations about the town. At midnight, the steamer leaves the port and morning finds us well out from shore on the Caribbean Sea.

Over forty years have passed, since I crossed the Isthmus by the Nicaragua route, but I readily recall the event and well remember the typographical features of the lake and river. I was 24 years old at that time and was not engaged at looking up routes for ship canals, but the survey of the Nicaragua Canal so many years later serves to bring the country through which it passes more prominent in my memory.

From Greytown to the head of the San Juan River, the canal survey follows the course of the river deviating from its course where prominent bends occur and shortens the distance by that much. Just above Castello is where the big locks are proposed to be built. Upon the South side the canal is to leave the lake about ten miles west of Virgin Bay and passes through Lake Managua leaving the cut upon that side less than five miles.

To me, the canal project looks to be a very feasible thing and the wonder is that the canal has not been built years ago. With the development of our western coast, of course the canal becomes more important to us, but it is not the United States alone that is to benefit. Like the Suez Canal, it will become the highway of all seagoing countries and will have a world-wide importance. If the millions that De Lesseps has squandered on his Panama scheme could have been expended upon this route, the canal would be in operation today and there would be no more vessels doubling Cape Horn and going 10,000 miles out of their way from New York to San Francisco or the Sandwich Islands.

Timber in the Atlantic states is getting nearly cut off and the price of lumber is getting to be exorbitant. While upon our western coast there are millions of acres of the finest timber that ever grew. Nearly worthless for want of a market. The Nicaragua Canal will open the way to the market and be of a universal benefit.

The "Northern Light" is a large boat and after being crowded for two weeks upon the "Pacific" and river boats, it seems a relief to get where we can have plenty of elbow room.

During the first three days' voyage, two of our passengers die, but nothing else occurs to mar the harmony of the trip. On the 4th day we sight the island of Cuba in the distance and vessels are frequently seen. The weather continues quite warm, but a good breeze makes things quite comfortable to those who are not driven to their berths by seasickness.

During the next three days we pass stormy weather without encountering a storm, which is unusual and unexpected, but the storm is waiting further on. On the morning of the 24th we wake to find ourselves tossing about on the foaming waves, the wind blowing a hurricane and the bow of the steamer turning landward. It is soon learned that the steamer has failed to get a supply of coal at Greytown and the stock on the boat is nearly exhausted.

The captain dares not take the risk of continuing on his way to New York during such a storm and tries to get into harbor in the Chesapeake Bay. As the day advances the gale increases in fury and the steamer can scarcely make headway against it. The wind is blowing directly off the shore with such force that no one can keep upon their feet on the deck and the fog is so dense at times that we cannot see the length of the boat. Guns are fired to signal pilots, but the storm has driven all the pilot boats into the harbor. Men are lashed to the wheelhouse continually throwing the lead, to get the soundings, and the shallowing of the water indicates that we are nearing the shore and are likely to strike upon a rock any moment.

While in this condition, the coal gives out. Small boats and everything combustible is broken up, and parts of the deck are taken up to keep up steam. To allow the steamer to drift out to sea in such a gale, without means of guiding it means sure destruction of the steamer and probable death to all the passengers and crew. All day we battle with the wind and waves and as night

61

comes on, it seems as if the steamer will be forced to relinquish the struggle and drift out to sea and left to the mercy of the waves.

The Captain, enveloped in tarpaulins, is in the pilot house with the wheelsman when one of the passengers makes his way across the deck and accosts the Captain by asking what the matter is. The Captain in his bluff manner replies, "Matter enough in trying to make a strange harbor in such a storm without a pilot and no means of keeping up steam."

The passenger informs him that years before he had been a pilot in the harbor, but the sands were constantly shifting, and he does not know anything about the present channel. The Captain tells him that if the passenger had ever been in the harbor, he had the advantage of himself and invites him into the pilot house, ordering tarpaulins for him and asking him to take charge of the boat.

The fog occasionally lifts a little while the passenger gets his bearings and he runs the steamer within 80 rods of the seashore of Cape Henry and orders the anchor dropped. Our provisions as well as coal are gone, and we have no supper that night and the only thing for dinner is cheese. Cheese is very good in its place, but it is not just the thing for a hungry man to make a hearty meal of.

During the night the storm abates, and we get wood from the shore in the morning and start up the bay to Norfolk. Ours is the first California steamer that had ever put into that port and as we near the wharf, we can see it fairly packed with curious people, but when the steamer strikes the wharf, not a person was visible. The sight of 1500 returning Californians in slouch hats, red and blue flannel shirts with revolvers strapped around them and handles of huge bowie knives in view impresses them with the notion that we are a hoard of pirates.

When we land and start up the streets, we find every building closed and the streets deserted. Three or four blocks ahead we see the woolly head of a darkey* peering around the corner, but long before we reach the place, the darkey has disappeared. By this time, we are getting pretty hungry and want some breakfast.

I am one of a party of about twenty that goes to one of the best hotels and asks for breakfast, but we're told that they cannot give us any. We notify the clerk that we are going to have something to eat if there is anything in the house, that we are not tramps or pirates and have money to pay for whatever we eat so he sets to work going into the kitchen and we soon have a good breakfast provided. The tables are filled during the entire day and before night comes, there is not an egg or chicken to be had in the city.

I am confident that is the most profitable day's business Norfolk has ever had. We not only eat up all the provisions of the town, but about four-fifths of the passengers celebrate perceptibly their landing upon the native shore by getting gloriously drunk and

63

(*pg 67)

quite a number of them end up in the cooler and were left there when the steamer leaves port.

I spend the day wandering about the streets and taking in the sights about the town and I am much pleased with the appearance of the city. There is a peculiarity about the residences which I have never noticed in any other town. Nearly all of them are built with a basement and the first or living floor is elevated about six feet above the pavement. To get into the houses, one must climb a side stairway six feet high. The streets are paved with cobble stones and if they had the traffic of some of our northern or western towns, the rattling of the wheels upon the pavement would be nearly deafening.

During the day, the steamer has put in coal and provisions and at noon, the lines are cast off and we steam into the harbor only to stick upon a sand bar where we remain for two or three hours. The Captain tries to roll the steamer off by getting all the passengers upon one side of the upper deck and at a signal all rush in a body to the other side. We try it several times and each time careen the steamer quite perceptibly but we're too hard aground to make the effort successful and have to await the rising of the tide before we get off.

The cold autumn winds drive all the passengers to their berths between decks where the air is foul and heated like an oven. On the morning of the 27th we steam into the harbor and cast the lines ashore at the company's wharf in New York.

64

I come out from my hot berth as yellow as a saffron bag with jaundice and feeling so badly that I can hardly get about. The health officer is almost persuaded to put me in quarantine as a yellow fever case but finally lets me go on shore.

I spend the day visiting the Crystal Palace and at night take the train, for home over the N.Y.C.R.R. (New York Central Railroad, established in 1853)

END

65

Image Credit:

*A note on racial colloquialisms

In the book there are several descriptions by the author that in today's vernacular would be considered racist statements (p. 63). Over one hundred and sixty seven years have elapsed since the time of these events, and the general views and experiences of Martin Noble Hine were vastly different from those of today. I hope this will be taken into consideration when reading.

I did not think it right to impose a censorship based on my own times and experience on this personal memoir and descriptive experience of a past time. Let the reader decide for themselves, based on the original text.

Thank you,

Adam Thompson

**Thank you to the readers of
California and Back: An 1850's Adventure!**

This is my first book and I am sincerely asking anyone who
enjoyed it if they would please take a second and review it
on Amazon! I can't tell you how grateful I am that you read
this little book and even more so for great reviews! I am so
excited to hear your thoughts!

Thank You,

Adam Thompson
Californiaandbackbook@gmail.com

Made in United States
Troutdale, OR
11/24/2023

14887068R00051